© PatrickGeorge 2021
First published in the United Kingdom in 2010
This revised edition published 2021

www.patrickgeorge.com

All rights reserved. No part of this publication may be reproduced or transmitted in any form or by any means, electronic or mechanical, including photocopying, recording or any information storage and retrieval system, without prior permission in writing from the publisher.

ISBN 978-0-9562558-9-1

3 5 7 9 10 8 6 4

British Library Cataloguing in Publication Data.
A catalogue record for this book is available from the British Library.

Printed in China.

OPPOSITES

patrickgeorge_illustration Patrick George

Big

Small

Sun

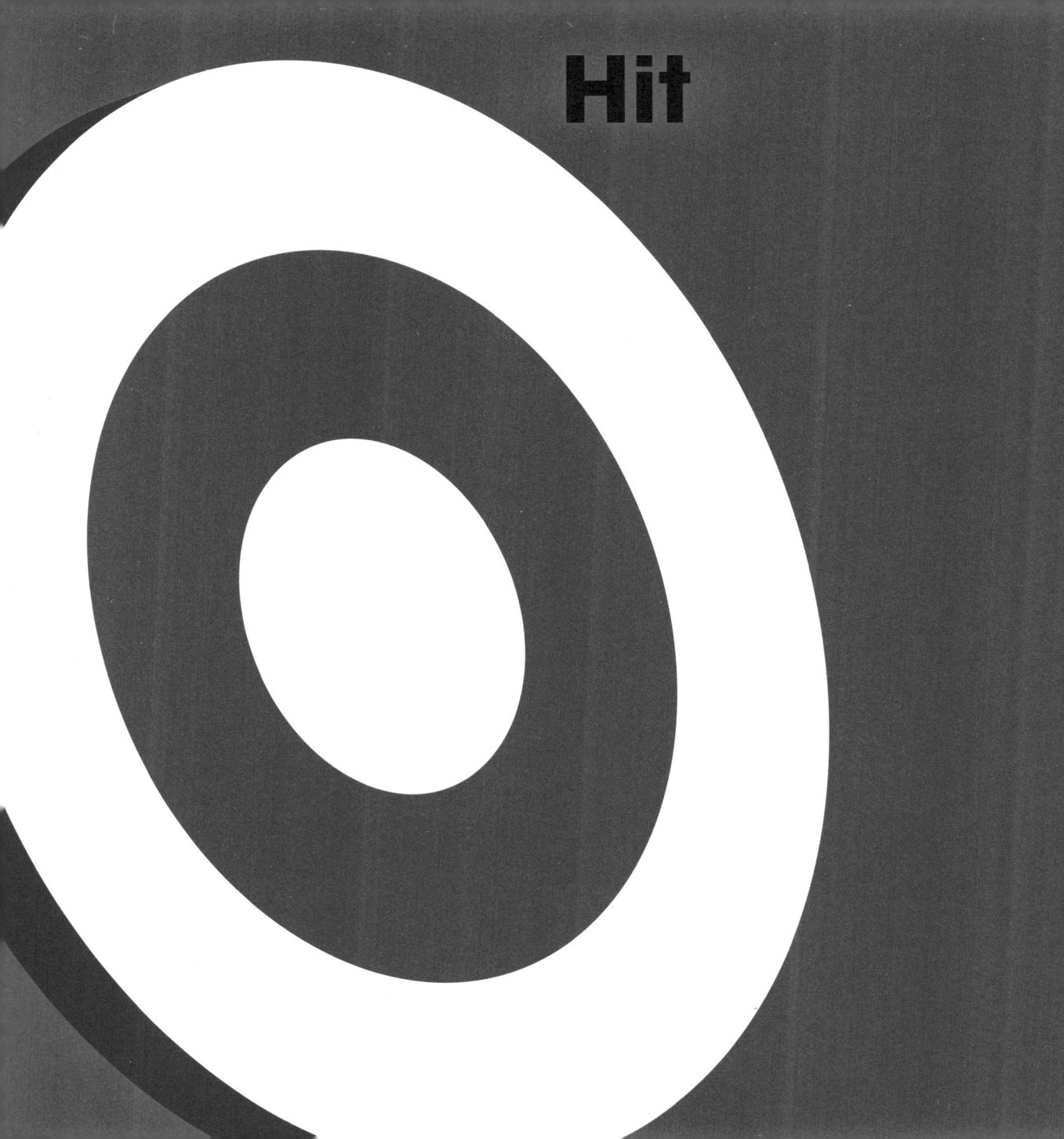

Miss

In

Out

Left

Right

Land

Sea

Boy

Girl

Hot

Cold

Empty

First

Last

Up

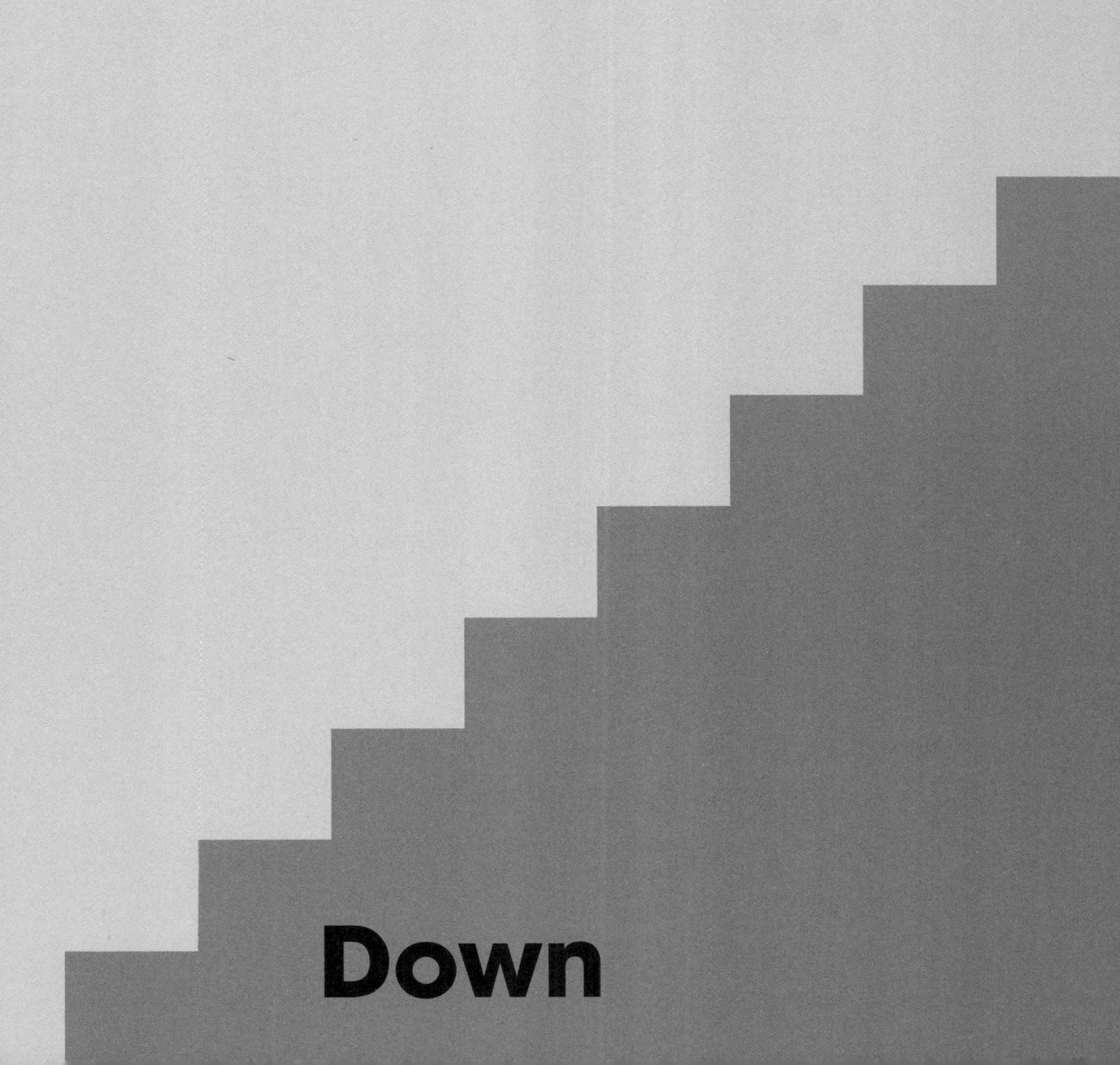